More SP⚽RTS BLOOPERS

More Weird, Wacky and Unexpected Moments in Sports

Phyllis and Zander Hollander

Illustrated with photographs

An Associated Features Book

SCHOLASTIC INC.
New York Toronto London Auckland Sydney

Photo Credits

Cover: (top) Wide World; (bottom) David Denoma/Wide World • 4, 6, 7: Wide World • 8: Sports Photo Source • 9: (top) Wide World; (bottom) UPI/Bettmann • 10, 11: Wide World • 12: New York Yankees • 13: Wide World • 14: George Gojkovich • 15: (top) Jonathan Kirn; (bottom) Richard Pilling • 16: UPI/Bettmann • 17: Ronald C. Modra • 18: UPI/Bettmann • 19: (top) Ronald C. Modra; (bottom) Wide World • 20: (top) Courtesy of Bob Wolff; (bottom) UPI/Bettmann • 21: (top) Sports Photo Source; (bottom) UPI/Bettmann • 22, 23: Wide World • 24: (top) UPI/Bettmann; (bottom) Wide World • 25, 26: UPI/Bettmann • 27–29: Wide World • 30: Sports Photo Source • 31: University of Maryland • 32: (top) Darryl Norenberg; (bottom) UPI/Bettmann • 33: Malcolm W. Emmons • 34: UPI/Bettmann • 35: Ringling Bros. and Barnum & Bailey Circus • 36: Michael Drazdzinski/University of Pittsburgh • 37: University of Iowa • 38: Bill Smith • 39: Tom Richards/Syracuse University • 40: UPI/Bettmann • 41: Wide World • 42: Courtesy of Herman L. Masin • 43: (top) David Denoma/Wide World; (bottom) Bowling Green State University • 44: (top) UPI/Bettmann; (bottom) Wide World • 45: Wide World • 46: (top) Yale University; (bottom left and right) Wide World • 47: (top; bottom left) Wide World; (bottom right) Yale University • 48: Courtesy of Jeff Iula • 49: (top) Courtesy of Herman L. Masin; (middle; bottom) Courtesy of Jeff Iula • 50: Rusty Kennedy/Wide World • 51: (top) Ringling Bros. and Barnum & Bailey Circus; (bottom) Barton Silverman • 52: Wide World • 53: Sports Photo Source • 54: (top) University of Louisville/Potter Collection; (bottom) Wide World • 55: (top) UPI/Bettmann; (bottom) Madison Square Garden • 56: Wide World • 57: (top) Anheuser Busch; (bottom) Wide World • 58: (top) Reuters/Bettmann; (bottom) Courtesy of Herman L. Masin • 59: (top) Wide World; (bottom) Minnesota Vikings • 60: (top) Wide World; (bottom) John Gaps/Wide World • 61–64: Wide World.

No part of this publication may be reproduced in whole or in part, or stored in a retrieval system, or transmitted in any form or by any means, electronic, mechanical, photocopying, recording, or otherwise, without written permission of the publisher. For information regarding permission, write to Scholastic Inc., 730 Broadway, New York, NY 10003.

ISBN 0-590-43873-5

Copyright © 1991 by Associated Features, Inc.
All rights reserved. Published by Scholastic Inc.

12 11 10 9 8 7 6 5 4 3 2 1   1 2 3 4 5 6/9

Printed in the U.S.A.   23

First Scholastic printing, March 1991

Contents

Introduction	5
Balanced Performer	6
Bee Day	7
Chicken Delight	7
Right for Dr. Strangeglove	8
Try It Just for Size	9
The Little Red Ping-Pong Machine	9
Where's the Ball?	10
Going, Going, Gone!	11
Mystery Man	12
Holy Cow!	13
Sledge Hitter	14
Beheaded	15
Broken Stick	15
Flight of the Curve	16
Double Tanana	17
A Full Plate	18
Bowling Night	18
"May I Have Your Autograph?"	19
The Misspelled Bat	19
Hold the Mustard!	20
Clowning Moment	20
"Lovely Hula Hands"	21
A Monstrous Occasion	21
Overheated	22
Silence, Please!	23
Blowing It	24
The Game's the Thing	24
A Mouthful	25
Wig Wag	26
Oops!	27
Look Out Below!	28
Gone to the Birds	29
Uplifting	30
High-Jump Layup	31
Nose Breaks	32
"Hey, Ref, I Shot It!"	34
Circus Shooters	35
Fractured Basket	36
No Whistle	37
The Refrigerator	38
Victory at Any Price	39
In Need of a Compass	40
Now Hear This!	41
The Never-Wilting Rose Bowl	42
A Kick That Counted	43
Flying Start	43
Ali's Strangest Match	44
The Grand Upset of Mike Tyson	44
Hi, Rocky	45
President Bush at Play	46
Soap Box Derby	48
No Stunt Photo	50
Monkeyshines	51
A Falling Sport	51
Oh, Chute!	52
There Is Always Hope	53
Whip Start	54
Where's the Jock?	54
Running for Life	55
Donkey Play	55
Ouch!	56
A Crowded Sea	57
Jackson to Jackson	57
What the Deuce!	58
Fashion of the Day	58
Super Frogs?	59
A Snaky Delivery	59
The Bicycle Kick	60
Caught in the Net	60
Cheers for Robin	61
Odyssey of the Eagle	62
The Giant and the Jockeys	63
Distressed Flag	64

Introduction

Welcome to another visit to the world of the unexpected in sports. This time you'll get to meet Greg Louganis, Bill Buckner, Sylvester Stallone, Michael Jackson, Bo Jackson, Andre the Giant, Hulk Hogan, Muhammad Ali, Ralph Sampson, Jerry West, Wilt Chamberlain, Buster Douglas, William "The Refrigerator" Perry, Ronald Reagan and Bob Hope, among others who have figured in the weird, wacky and strange moments of games played across the American landscape and around the world.

You'll see Robin Williams as a Denver Broncos cheerleader, Hank Aaron dumping Tim McCarver, Frank Robinson wearing a wig, Mike Tyson flat on his back, President George Bush catching a fish and Jimmy Connors eating his tennis racquet.

You'll encounter a zoo of characters, ranging from a snake that didn't disturb an NFL coach, swarming bees that stopped a baseball game, the San Diego Chicken doing his thing, a less-than-holy cow that responded to Phil Rizzuto and oversized frogs that leapt at a chance to compete in the Frog Jump Jubilee.

You'll wonder at a mystery player who wound up in a New York Yankee uniform and a parachutist who dared to descend on a World Series game.

It all adds up to a circus of sports, including monkeys on a motorcycle, hoopsters on unicycles, a baseball player blowing bubble gum as he tries to put the tag on an opponent, and a major-league manager who tackles what may have been the world's biggest hot dog.

Ahead is an all-star cast of athletes, actors, comedians and others who wittingly or unwittingly made possible *More Sports Bloopers*.

— *Phyllis and Zander Hollander*

Balanced Performer

Julio Cruz was a second baseman who played for more than a decade in the major leagues. He made it with his glove, but he liked to perform a balancing act with a bat and ball. As a member of the Chicago White Sox, he demonstrates during batting practice before a 1983 game against the Kansas City Royals.

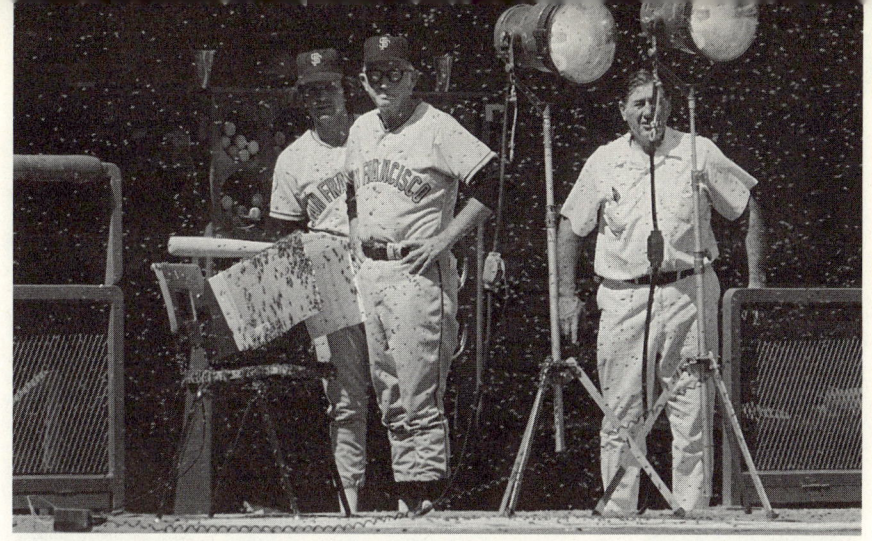

Bee Day

The San Francisco Giants have endured an earthquake (1989 World Series) and the winds of Candlestick Park over the years. But they encountered something of another nature in a 1976 game at Cincinnati's Riverfront Stadium. A swarm of bees descended onto the field. The best catcher on the field was Cincinnati's Johnny Bench. But he didn't catch bees. Professional beekeepers were beeped via 911, and the game was delayed until the queen bee was captured.

Chicken Delight

The San Diego Chicken, Ted Giannoulas, found a target in Cincinnati Reds catcher Alex Trevino between innings of a 1983 exhibition game against the Minnesota Twins at Minneapolis. Trevino didn't cluck with approval when he was upended by the Chicken.

Right for Dr. Strangeglove

Dick Stuart was such a poor-fielding first baseman that he was given the nickname "Dr. Strangeglove" when he played for the Pittsburgh Pirates in the late 1950s. Would he have been helped if he'd had this glove? Made of steel, it's 12 feet high and weighs 5,800 pounds. The sculptor was Claes Oldenburg.

Try It Just for Size

Jimmy Rooney was a nine-year-old from Newburyport, Massachusetts, when he took the field with this glove in 1978. It's two feet tall, weighs 10 pounds and was autographed by such famous players as Babe Ruth and Bob Feller. It's more than 60 years old and is a Rooney family heirloom. Jimmy's grandfather bought the glove for $10 and occasionally displayed it in his hardware store.

The Little Red Ping-Pong Machine

In the mid-1970s, the World Champion Cincinnati Reds were known as "The Big Red Machine." They also had what could be called "The Little Red Ping-Pong Machine," comprised of sons of the players. The kids are Pete Rose, Jr. (14); Tony Perez's boys, Victor (24) and Eduardo (right foreground); and Cesar Geronimo, Jr., atop the table. The big leaguer watching them is Cesar Geronimo.

Where's the Ball?

The Oakland A's Dave Kingman hit a high pop-up against Minnesota's Frank Viola at the Metrodome in Minneapolis on May 4, 1984. Twins third baseman John Castino (2) and shortstop Houston Jimenez waited for the ball to come down. It never did. The ball disappeared through a drainage hole in the Metrodome's fabric ceiling, about 180 feet above home plate. Umpire Jim Evans gave Kingman a ground-rule double for his hole-in-one.

Going, Going, Gone!

Outfielders customarily climb the walls in pursuit of long drives. That was the aim of Kansas City Royals outfielder Dan Garcia in a 1981 exhibition game against the Pittsburgh Pirates at Bradenton, Florida. Garcia not only didn't spear the ball (a home run by Mike Easler), but in the process he lost his glove over the fence.

Mystery Man

These were the 1927 World Champion New York Yankees. The circled player next to Babe Ruth is listed as Don Miller in the official caption that accompanies the photo. But who is Don Miller? Nobody knows. Don Miller never played for the Yankees; in fact, *The Baseball Encyclopedia* has no Don Miller. Perhaps he was a friend of Ruth's and they did it for a gag. It remains a mystery after all these years.

Front row (from left): Julie Wera, Mike Gazella, Pat Collins, Eddie Bennett (mascot), Benny Bengough, Ray Morehart, Myles Thomas, Cedric Durst. *Middle row:* Urban Shocker, Joe Dugan, Earle Combs, Charlie O'Leary (coach), Miller Huggins (manager), Art Fletcher (coach), Mark Koenig, Dutch Ruether, Johnny Grabowski, George Pipgras. *Back row:* Lou Gehrig, Herb Pennock, Tony Lazzeri, Wilcy Moore, Babe Ruth, Don Miller, Bob Meusel, Bob Shawkey, Waite Hoyt, Joe Giard, Ben Paschal, (unknown), Doc Wood (trainer).

Holy Cow!

As a player and announcer, Phil "Scooter" Rizzuto has been with the New York Yankees for more than half a century. He was a pint-sized shortstop (5-foot-6, 150 pounds) known for his bunting skills and peerless fielding. As an announcer, his trademark expression is "Holy Cow." When the Yankees retired his number 10 on Rizzuto Day at Yankee Stadium, he was given a number of gifts, including a cow (above). Whereupon the cow, making like a base-runner attempting to steal second, upended Rizzuto (below). Holy cow!

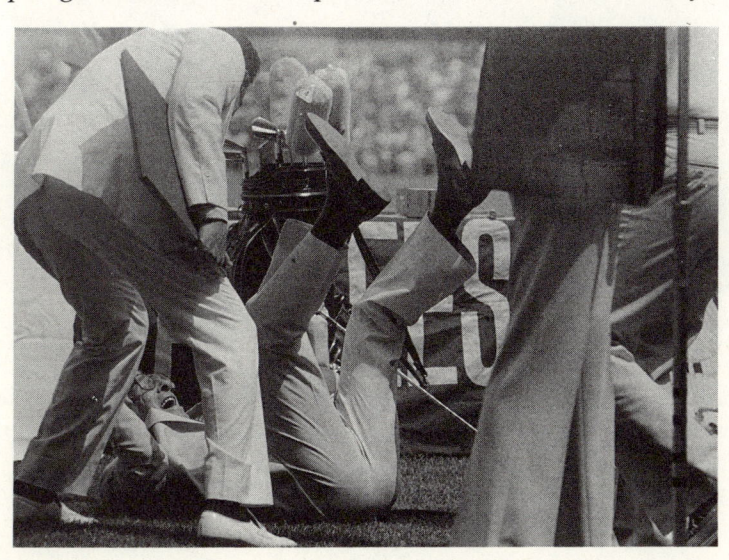

Sledge Hitter

Baseball players swing two, sometimes three bats, or use a leaded donut on a bat before they take batting practice or go to the plate in a game. It makes the bat feel lighter when it counts. But Barry Bonds of the Pittsburgh Pirates uses a sledgehammer. If you can lift it, try it.

Beheaded

Players sometimes lose their heads emotionally in the heat of a game. There was no emotion involved here. The White Sox' Luis Salazar ducked an inside pitch in a 1986 game, and the photographer, not the pitcher, beheaded him at the precise moment.

Broken Stick

Cesar Cedeno of the St. Louis Cardinals follows through with perfect form after breaking his bat in the 1985 World Series against the Kansas City Royals.

Flight of the Curve

Lee Strange was a 10-year major-league pitcher with the Twins, Indians, Red Sox and White Sox. Later, as a Red Sox pitching coach in 1974, he demonstrated this flight of his curveball. The photo was taken at the rate of 120 frames per second by Dr. Harold E. Edgerton, an MIT professor, and was exhibited in Boston's Museum of Science.

Double Tanana

Photographer Ronald Modra did this multiple exposure of Frank Tanana, pitching for the California Angels in the 1970s.

A Full Plate

Were the Pirates ganging up on the Mets? In a 1964 game, Dick Schofield was about to take his cut at the plate while on-deck batter Bob Bailey prepared to do the same. The Mets catcher was Jesse Gonder; the umpire, Ken Burkhart.

Bowling Night

The Atlanta Braves' Hank Aaron (right) not only hit homers, he hit catchers. In a 1969 game, Hank bowls over St. Louis Cardinal catcher Tim McCarver to score on a sacrifice fly.

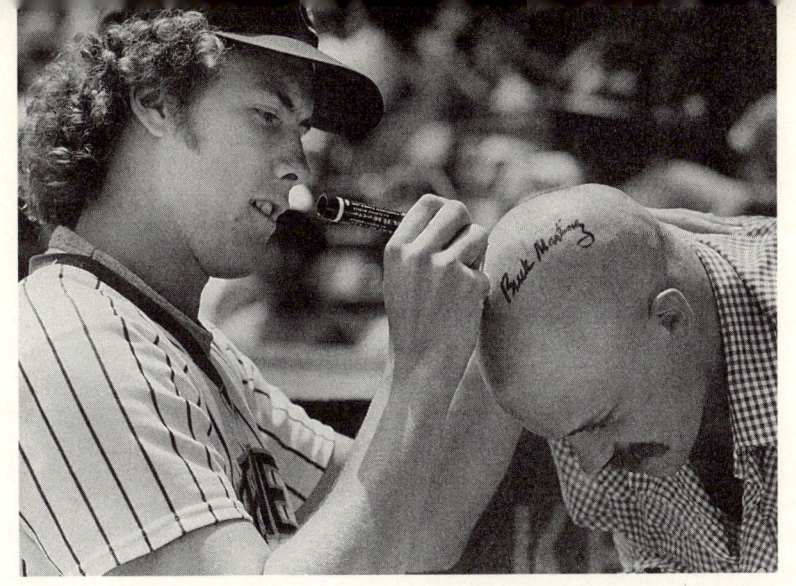

"May I Have Your Autograph?"

Players sign their name on anything from baseball cards, balls and programs to . . . well, a bald head. In this instance in 1979, Milwaukee Brewer pitcher Lary Sorensen responds to a request for his autograph. Teammate Buck Martinez had preceded him. Presumably the fan didn't shower for weeks thereafter.

The Misspelled Bat

Oakland Athletics catcher Terry Steinbach did everything right in the 1988 All-Star Game. His home run and sacrifice fly accounted for all the runs in the American League's 2–1 victory over the National League. But Terry's bat was something else. The manufacturer misspelled his name as Steinbech. See it, although barely discernible, under "Big Stick." So after the game, he autographed it correctly.

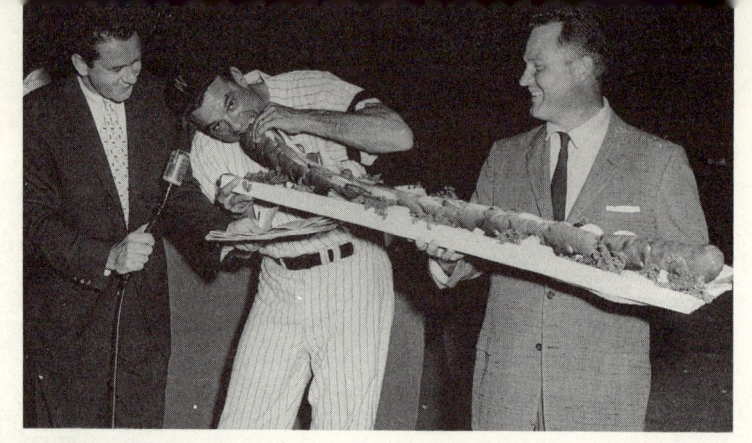

Hold the Mustard!

Cookie Lavagetto's greatest years were as a Brooklyn Dodger third baseman, and his most dramatic contribution occurred in the fourth game of the 1947 World Series against the New York Yankees. Pinch-hitting with two out in the ninth, Cookie hit the game-winning two-run double that broke up Bill Bevens's no-hit game. His next-biggest challenge may have been when he was managing the Washington Senators in 1958. He was given this seven-foot frankfurter. Announcer Bob Wolff did the play-by-play as Cookie attacked the dog.

Clowning Moment

In the days when there was a team in the nation's capital, Washington Senators pitchers Al Schacht (right) and Nick Altrock enlivened the proceedings with their antics. Schacht, who was known as the "Clown Prince of Baseball," and his partner led the band before a game in 1925.

"Lovely Hula Hands"

Promotions to lure the fans have long been a side feature of baseball. It all began in the minor leagues, and today, in the majors as well as the minors, there are all sorts of giveaways, exhibitions and fan-participation contests. These range from "Kiss the Pig" to "Teenage Mutant Ninja Turtle Night" to "Lady Dynamite," who appears to blow herself up. The minor leaguers pictured here performed at a "Hula Night."

A Monstrous Occasion

A whale? The Loch Ness monster? It's an infield tarpaulin that nearly took off when the winds blew mightily at a 1968 game at Yankee Stadium. Rather than resort to harpoons, the ground crew held on, as they might to a runaway balloon, and finally got the tarp down to the turf.

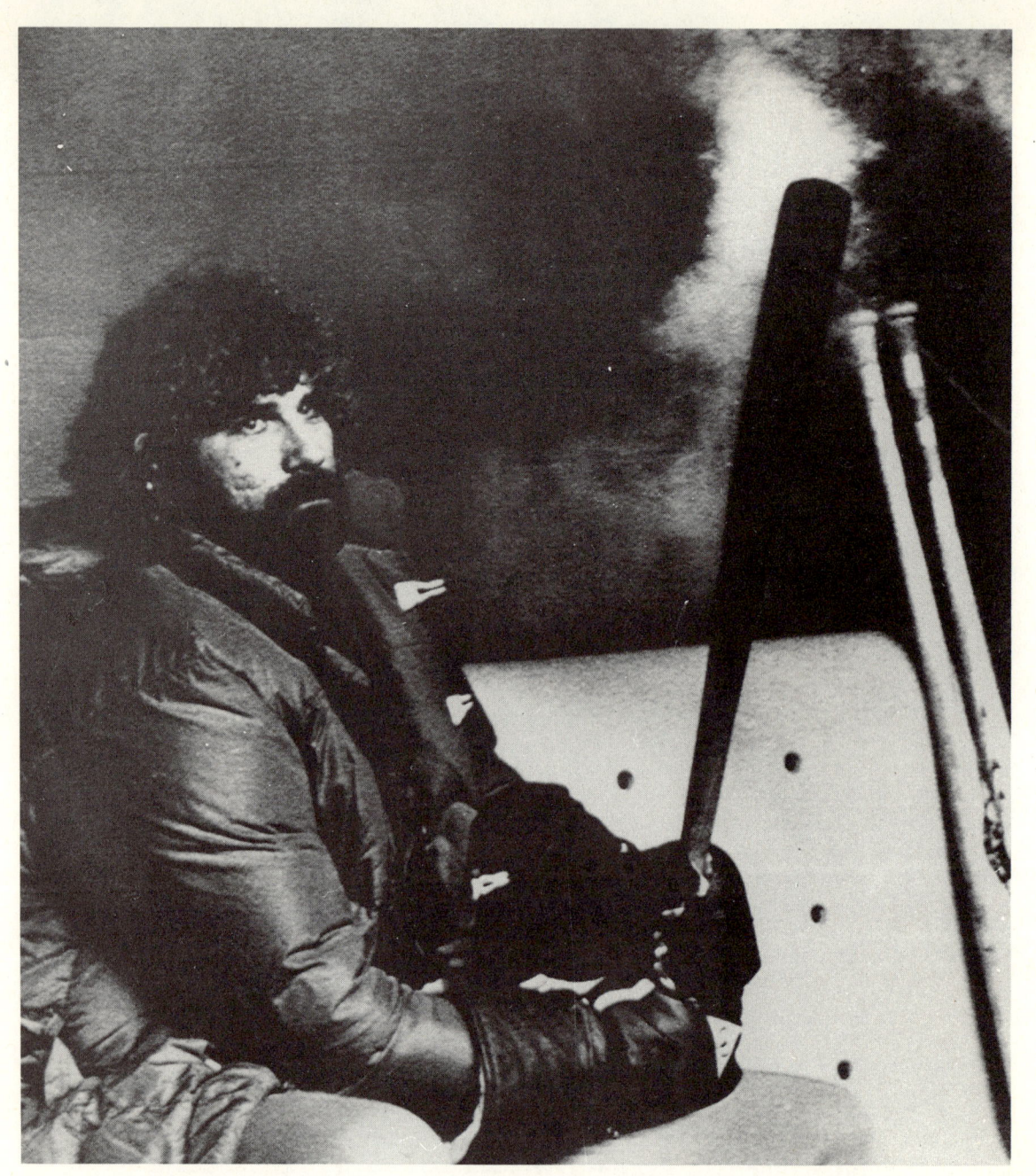

Overheated

It was a cold night in September 1980 when Pete Vuckovich, a St. Louis Cardinals pitcher who was hitting .183 at the time, put his bat into a dugout heater. The result was this smoking bat. It didn't help his average, but it warmed him up.

Silence, Please!

Normally vocal Dave Parker, who loved to insult friends and foes alike, stepped out of character before a Pittsburgh-Montreal game in 1979. After one of his teammates told him to shut up, Parker put a piece of tape across his mouth. It didn't last long. He removed it before getting back to his familiar heckling.

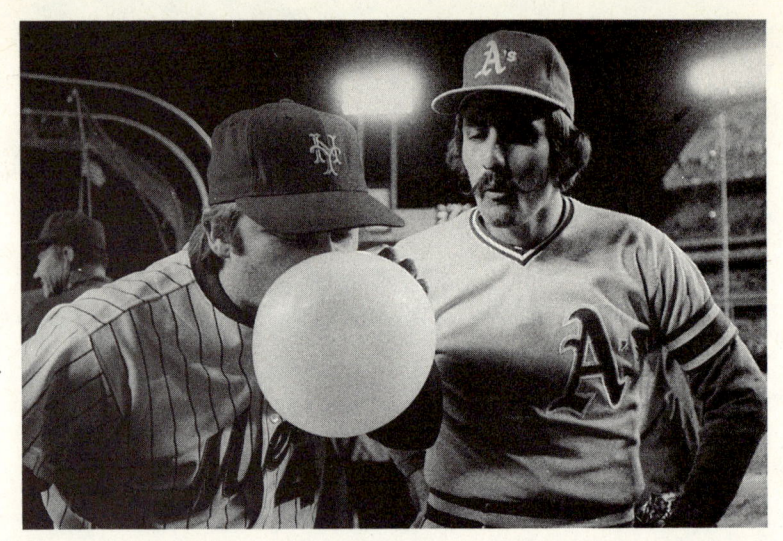

Blowing It

The Oakland A's Rollie Fingers watches as rival reliever Tug McGraw of the New York Mets demonstrates at the 1973 World Series. Although McGraw won a game and wound up with a 2.63 earned-run average, the bubble burst for the Mets when the A's took the Series in seven games.

The Game's the Thing

Can you blow bubble gum and play baseball at the same time? You can, but the result may not be a happy one, as Pittsburgh Pirate second baseman Jim Morrison discovered in a 1983 game against the San Diego Padres. Luis Salazar was safe on the play.

A Mouthful

Luscious Luke Easter didn't lose a tooth or break his nose on this one in a game between the Cleveland Indians and the Philadelphia A's in 1950. The Indian first baseman is sliding home on a sacrifice fly as the ball bounces out of A's catcher Mickey Guerra's glove.

Wig Wag

They called it a "kangaroo court," in which mock trials were held for players up on all sorts of charges. It was a humorous interlude for the Baltimore Orioles in 1969 when Frank Robinson, then a star outfielder, wore the magistrate's wig as the permanent judge. Guilty players had to pay modest fines that went into a fund used for worthy causes. Robinson doesn't wear the wig anymore. It was replaced by the managerial cap of his old team, the Orioles.

Oops!

Boston Red Sox first baseman Bill Buckner is a picture of dejection as he leaves the field after committing an error that allowed the winning run to score in the 10th inning of the sixth game of the 1986 World Series against the Mets. The error came when Mookie Wilson's grounder rolled through Buckner's legs. The Mets went on to capture the Series, and Buckner was enshrined as Goat of the Year.

Look Out Below!

When it rains, it pours — or so Oakland A's outfielder Billy North discovered in a 1977 game against the Minnesota Twins. A flock of sea gulls invaded Oakland Coliseum, and North put his glove on his head to protect himself from the droppings.

Gone to the Birds

From the earliest days, youngsters playing ball on their local fields have had to contend with the stray dog, or cat, who interrupts a game. It has happened in the minor leagues, and once in a while in the majors. But a bird? Well, home-plate umpire Harry Wendelstedt, the big bully, had to shoo one away when it stopped play at a 1985 game between the Philadelphia Phillies and the Los Angeles Dodgers.

Uplifting

Ralph Sampson of the University of Virginia was the best center prospect in college basketball in 1982–83. In the 1983 NBA draft, he became the first pick, selected by the Houston Rockets. But some questioned whether Sampson's skinny frame could take the pounding of the pros. With the help of Bill Dunn, Virginia's strength and conditioning coach, Sampson underwent a weight-lifting regimen and read Dunn's book, *Strength Training and Conditioning for Basketball*. One result: He could lift the burly Dunn. Another: Sampson withstood it all and became a dominant figure with the Rockets until injuries took their toll.

High-Jump Layup

Frank Costello of the University of Maryland was the national indoor high-jump champion in 1965. On a dare, he took a stab at trying to make a layup with his feet. Did he make it? Who knows? But it's one freaky shot.

Nose Breaks

During Jerry West's 13-year Hall of Fame career with the Los Angeles Lakers, he suffered a broken nose countless times. Whatever the number, he is assured of having the unofficial NBA record in this department.

Dolph Schayes was a superstar center for more than 15 years with the Syracuse Nationals. He made the All-NBA first team six times and wound up in the Basketball Hall of Fame. He wore this face mask in 1962 after someone broke his beak.

Wilt Chamberlain towered over all in his 14 years in the NBA with the Philadelphia and San Francisco Warriors, the Philadelphia 76ers and the Los Angeles Lakers. Among his many records are a 100-point game and 4,029 points in a single season, the only player ever to surpass the 4,000-point mark. He needed the mask in 1965 when he was with the 76ers.

"Hey, Ref, I Shot It!"

Does the unidentified referee here get credit for the basket? It may look like he shot it, but it was tossed by the Baltimore Bullets' Kevin Loughery (right) in a 1971 NBA playoff game against the New York Knickerbockers.

Circus Shooters

The King Charles Troupe combined basketball prowess and unicycle wizardry at the Ringling Bros. and Barnum & Bailey Circus.

Fractured Basket

Before high-flying Jerome Lane of the University of Pittsburgh became a first-round draft pick of the Denver Nuggets in 1988, he demolished the basket on a slam dunk against Providence.

No Whistle

Larry Mikan, son of the great George Mikan, never matched his dad's achievements as a professional, but as a University of Minnesota collegian he displayed this defensive maneuver against Iowa in 1970. Somehow the officials didn't call him on the rejection, so the basket didn't count. It didn't matter because Iowa won the game en route to a perfect Big Ten season.

The Refrigerator

When 310-pound William Perry burst across the TV screens of America on *Monday Night Football* on October 21, 1985, he rocked the Richter scale. As a rookie defensive tackle for the Chicago Bears, he became an instant offensive hero with massive blocks that led to two touchdowns and then his own touchdown run against the Green Bay Packers. Two weeks later, again against Green Bay, the big Bear caught his first touchdown pass and a nation of fans went wild. He was nicknamed "The Refrigerator" when he was an All-America at Clemson College, where he was "350 pounds and rising."

Victory at Any Price

What the well-dressed quarterback wears. Syracuse University's Tom Woodruff paid the price in sartorial splendor when he emerged after leading his team to a 28–24 triumph over West Virginia in 1971.

In Need of a Compass

The San Francisco-Minnesota game at San Francisco on October 25, 1964, featured one of the greatest goof-ups in NFL history. The Vikings' Jim Marshall scooped up 49er Billy Kilmer's fumble (top) and, looking back to see if any foe was near him (bottom, left), ran 60 yards in the wrong direction, giving San Francisco a two-point safety. Having scored for the 49ers, he was congratulated by San Francisco's Bruce Bosley (bottom, right). But the Vikings won the game, 27–22.

Now Hear This!

Testing, 1–2–3. San Francisco 49er quarterback Steve DeBerg, suffering from a throat ailment, used a small microphone taped to his face mask for a game against the St. Louis Cardinals in 1980. A small amplifier enabled his signal-calling to be audible to his teammates. The 49ers got the message. They emerged with a 24–21 overtime victory.

The Never-Wilting Rose Bowl

It has been almost a century since the first Rose Bowl Game in 1902 and more than 100 years since the birth of the colorful Tournament of Roses parade. The game's the thing, but so is the spectacle that precedes it in Pasadena, California.

It's not the Goodyear blimp, but it's ready for take-off in the 1919 Tournament of Roses.

The cover of the 1912 Tournament of Roses parade program.

This ticket was for the only Rose Bowl game never played in the Rose Bowl. Oregon and Duke were to play in Pasadena on New Year's Day, January 1, 1942, but World War II began on December 7, 1941, with the bombing of Pearl Harbor by the Japanese. The game was switched to Durham, North Carolina, because it was feared that California might be the next target.

A Kick That Counted

It looks like a kick in the pants for Purdue's Steve Jackson from Ohio State placekicker Pat O'Marrow in a 1989 game at Ohio Stadium. Actually, O'Marrow is following through on an extra point while the Boilermakers' Jackson gets spun around by a blocker. There was no connection.

Flying Start

The Flying Falcons of Bowling Green unleashed an aerial star in Dave Turner in this 1970s game against Kent State. He was offside. Both Turner and Bowling Green came down to earth as Kent State upset the Falcons, 14–10.

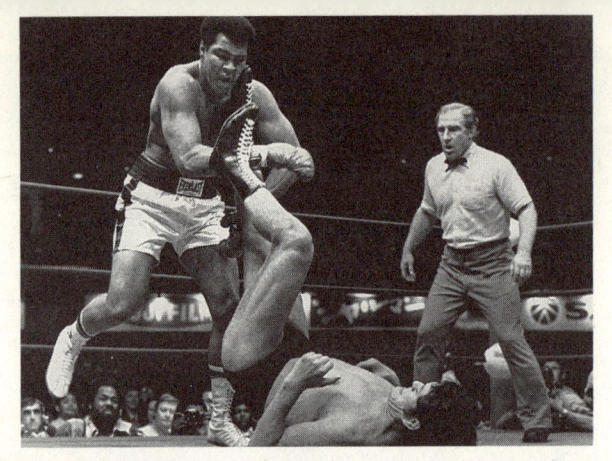

Ali's Strangest Match

It was an exhibition match: Fighter vs. Wrestler. Muhammad Ali, then three-time heavyweight boxing champion, vs. Antonio Inoki, Japanese wrestling champion. It took place on July 26, 1976, in Tokyo. Ali would fight; his opponent would wrestle. Inoki lay on the mat like a crab, kicking his legs out at Ali, who kept circling as he looked for an opening. The spectacle lasted 15 rounds and was called a draw.

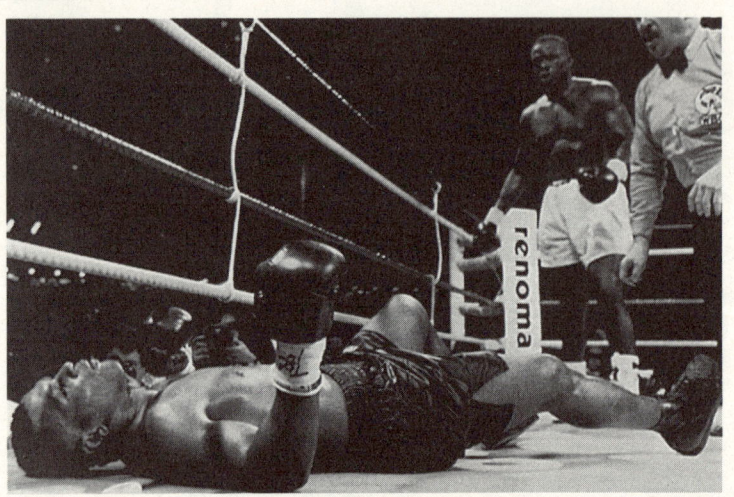

The Grand Upset of Mike Tyson

Mike Tyson was considered the unbeatable heavyweight champion when he met James "Buster" Douglas, a decided underdog, in a title match on February 11, 1990, in Tokyo. But Douglas rebounded from an eight-round knockdown to knock out Tyson in the 10th round and win the title. It was one of the biggest upsets in boxing history. Tyson had never lost a professional fight, and 33 of his 37 victories were by knockout.

Hi, Rocky

Actor Sylvester Stallone, as Rocky, contemplates towering wrestler Hulk Hogan, as Thunderlips, in *Rocky III*. They threw each other out of the ring, and the referee called it a draw. It was only a movie.

President Bush at Play

In the United States, sports have been a national tradition, and most of the Presidents have set an example. George Bush may well be the most sporting president in history. He plays golf, tennis, softball and horseshoes; he hunts, fishes, jogs and swims.

Bush was captain and first baseman at Yale.

He's a skilled horseshoe pitcher.

Bush swings away in a softball game between the White House staff and the press corps in Kennebunk, Maine.

After weeks of frustration, the President finally catches a bluefish off the waters of his Maine retreat (above). His mother was an outstanding junior tennis player, and Bush has been wielding a racquet since he was five years old (below left). In the spring of the year he died, 1948, Babe Ruth presented the future President with a copy of his autobiography at Yale (below right).

Soap Box Derby

It all began after a news photographer, Myron Scott of the Dayton (Ohio) *Daily News*, encountered three boys racing homemade, engineless cars on an inclined street. Scott was inspired to set up a more formal race and out of that came the first Soap Box Derby, in Dayton on August 19, 1933. There were 362 entries, with cars built on orange crates, sheet tin, wagon and baby-buggy wheels and almost anything else of "junk value." The race, later to be called the All-American Soap Box Derby, was staged the next year in Akron, Ohio, and it has been an August tradition ever since, with entries from around the nation and the world. The nationally televised event has drawn celebrity spectators from the entertainment, sports and political worlds, ranging from actor Jimmy Stewart to athletes O.J. Simpson and Oscar Robertson to Ronald Reagan and Richard Nixon. Some of them have participated in a special supplementary event known as the Oil-Can Race, in which they compete on the 954-foot strip in specially built oversized cars. For them, it is a fun thing. For the serious, young competitors, it is their equivalent of the Indy 500.

The first champion, in 1933, was Bob Gravett of Dayton, Ohio.

Joe Lunn of Columbus, Georgia, won in 1952.

Jack Dempsey, the former heavyweight boxing champion, took third in the first Oil-Can Race, in 1950. The winner was Wilbur Shaw, three-time Indy 500 champion, followed by actor Jimmy Stewart.

Ronald Reagan entered the 1951 Oil-Can Race. Curiously, the conventional car behind him has a license that reads DC 1. Three decades later, DC 1 would symbolize the Washington, DC, plate of Ronald Reagan, President of the United States. The DC actually stood for the name of Dave Corbin, the sponsoring Chevrolet agency owner.

Darwin Cooper (second from right), the 1951 Derby winner, is congratulated by Ronald Reagan as actor Andy Devine (right) and ventriloquist Paul Winchell, with dummy Jerry Mahoney, look on. In their Oil-Can Race, the team of Winchell and Mahoney was the winner, with Reagan second and Devine third. Reagan quipped afterward: "I lost to a dummy."

No Stunt Photo

Rusty Kennedy, a Philadelphia photographer, captured this crash in a 1989 NASCAR race. The photo was selected as the action-category winner in the annual Associated Press sports editors contest.

Monkeyshines

Mickey Antalek's super chimps were featured motorcyclists in the Ringling Bros. and Barnum & Bailey Circus.

A Falling Sport

It was called the Roller Derby, a mixture of elbow-swinging, mayhem-bent roller skaters who had their heyday in the 1950s and early sixties. Five-person teams opposed each other (men and women separately), and they whirled around a banked wooden track in big arenas like New York's Madison Square Garden and armories across the nation. A point was scored each time a player passed an opponent after circling the track. Spinning, pushing, shoving and body-blocking were standard, and many observers likened the violence and theatrics to professional wrestling. Once popular on television, the Roller Derby gradually faded from the "sporting" scene. Here one of the women takes a spill at Madison Square Garden.

Oh, Chute!

Fans and players were shocked during the first inning of the sixth game of the 1986 World Series when a man parachuted onto the field at New York's Shea Stadium. He was identified as Michael Sergio. The police arrested him.

There Is Always Hope

As a young comedian, Bob Hope took to golf after he gave up the sport of boxing. He has played with Presidents and pros, and with humor, as is evident from this shot at a tournament in the 1950s in Westbury, New York.

Whip Start

The starter at the left cracked a whip to get the horses off and running in the 1914 Kentucky Derby. It wasn't until 1930 that a stall machine came into use and eliminated the need for the whip.

Where's the Jock?

A riderless horse named Schoeller clears the final jump in the 1979 Bolla Steeplechase at Louisville, Kentucky. He had previously dumped his jockey. Next to him is Toinette Jackson aboard Owhata Chief. Schoeller went on to finish first but was disqualified because there has to be a jockey aboard.

Running for Life

A four-horse chariot gives chase to a "Roman" during the Festa Italiana at New York's Madison Square Garden in 1966. Chariot races were the sport of the wealthy during the days of the Roman Empire.

Donkey Play

This girl with her donkey lent a humorous touch to the 1970 National Horse Show at Madison Square Garden.

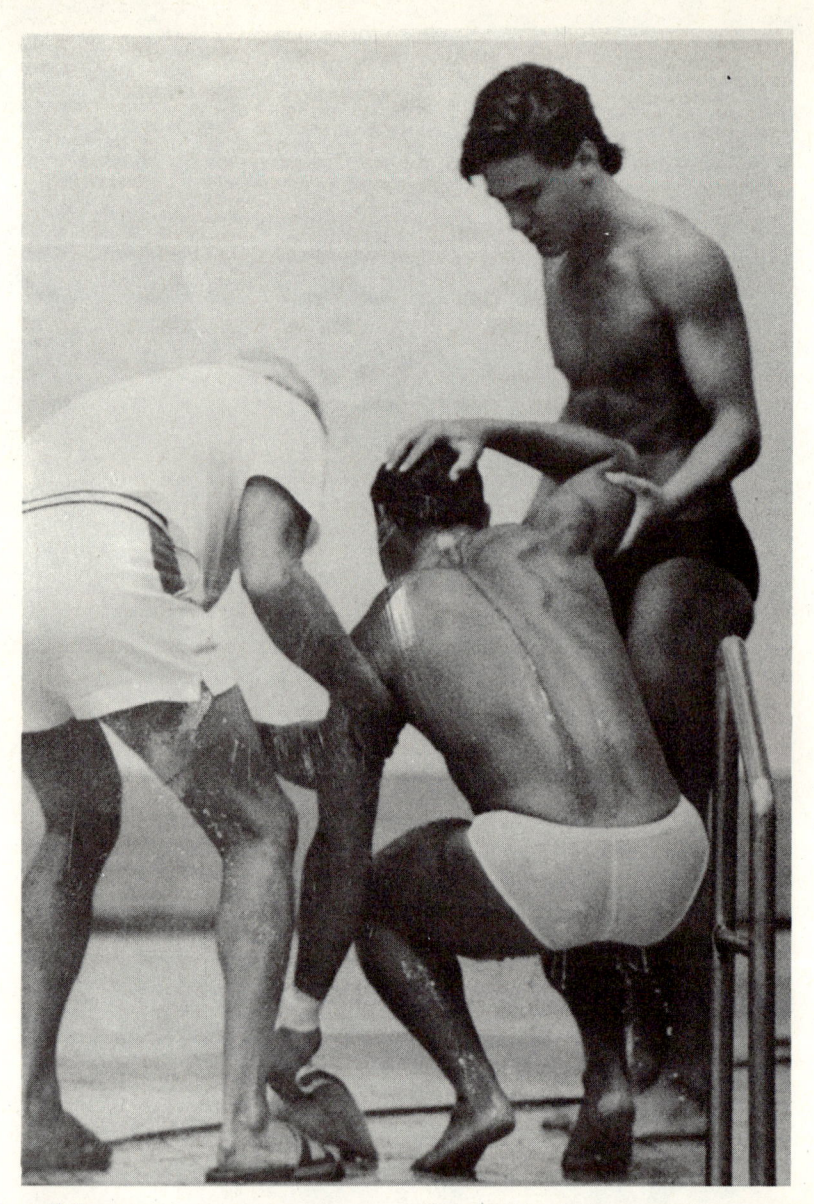

Ouch!

Even the world's greatest divers miss — or hit, as is the case with Greg Louganis of the U.S. at the 1988 Olympic Games in Seoul, Korea. Greg is being assisted after nipping his head on the springboard preliminaries while doing a reverse 2½ somersault. He suffered a nasty gash, but came back to win the event and also take a second gold medal in platform diving.

A Crowded Sea

A flood of 1,275 swimmers representing 39 countries and 50 states competed in the 1988 Bud Light Ironman Triathlon World Championship at Kailua-Kona, Hawaii. They are navigating a 2.4-mile ocean swim. The other events in this grueling event were a 112-mile bike ride and a 26.2-mile marathon run.

Jackson to Jackson

Michael Jackson fakes a pass to Bo Jackson of the Los Angeles Raiders and Kansas City Royals at Michael's recording studio in Los Angeles. The two-sport superstar gave Michael an autographed football and baseball. There was no indication Michael would take up either sport.

What the Deuce!

Jimmy Connors entertains the crowd after missing a shot to Israel's Gilad Bloom in the 1989 Riklis Classic at Tel Aviv. Connors dropped the first set in the finals, but went on to win the title.

Fashion of the Day

These young sprinters were fashionable in the 1920s. They were also fast. (From left) Madeline Adams, Grace Rittler, Dorothy Baugh and Frances Ruppert were the Meadowbrook foursome that set a women's world record 52.4 seconds in the 440-yard relay at a meet in New York.

Super Frogs?

Andy Koffman, a Seattle importer of exotic birds, reptiles and amphibians, displays six of the giant frogs captured in Cameroon, Africa. They measured up to three feet long, and the biggest weighed 15 pounds. Koffman made some people hopping mad when he entered them in the 1990 Frog Jump Jubilee, held annually in Angels Camp, California, and inspired by Mark Twain's *The Celebrated Jumping Frog of Calaveras County*. Koffman estimated his frogs could easily exceed, in a single bound, the contest record of 21 feet, 5¾ inches, achieved in three hops by Rosie the Ribiter in 1986. As it turned out, none of Koffman's frogs came close. His jumpingest frog finished in 63rd place. It would have delighted Mark Twain.

A Snaky Delivery

There were those who only saw Bud Grant as "The Great Stone Face" when he was on the sidelines as coach of the Minnesota Vikings in the NFL. But off the field he was a practical joker. A naturalist and fisherman, he was known for placing salamanders in desk drawers of the Viking secretaries, and once he smuggled a rooster into the ladies' room. But the women turned the tables on him one day. They borrowed a 10-foot python from the Minneapolis Zoo and placed it on Grant's desk. Cool as a coach with a 50-point lead in the Super Bowl, Grant wrapped the python around his neck and went about his business.

The Bicycle Kick

Pele, generally considered the greatest soccer player of all time, perfected this bicycle kick during a career that took him from his native Brazil to Europe and to New York, where he was the magnetic force of the Cosmos in the North American Soccer League.

Caught in the Net

This young soccer goalie in Des Moines, Iowa, not only yielded a goal but also got snared in the net. Photographer John Gaps III captured the scene in 1989, and his shot won first place in the photo-feature category of the Associated Press Sports Editors contest.

Cheers for Robin

Robin "Mork" Williams became a cheerleader for a day when he joined the Denver Broncos Pony Express squad for a 1979 episode of the *Mork and Mindy* television series. This was at Denver's Mile High Stadium.

Odyssey of the Eagle

Eddie "The Eagle" Edwards, a part-time plasterer from North Chelthenham, England, became a sudden celebrity at the 1988 Winter Olympics in Calgary, Canada. There are no snow-capped mountains in England, and he'd only taken up ski-jumping two years earlier. But he became Great Britain's lone Olympic entry in the sport. Athletes from other nations responded to the inexperienced 24-year-old's freestyle approach to life and helped him with equipment and instruction. He was at best ungainly, but he had courage and enthusiasm. Soon there were "Eddie the Eagle" T-shirts, and he appeared on *The Tonight Show* with Johnny Carson. The crowd rooted for him at Calgary, but alas, "Eddie the Eagle" landed 58th out of 58 entries in the 70-meter jump and 55th out of 55 in the 90-meter.

The Giant and the Jockeys

Professional wrestler Andre the Giant was overmatched when he met jockeys Richard Privitera (hoisted), Nick Santagata (left) and Wesley Ward at New York's Aqueduct Race Track in 1985. The wrestler is 7-foot-4 and weighs 492 pounds. "He picked me up like a bag of potato chips," said the 90-pound Privitera.

Distressed Flag

The flag was familiar but something was wrong. This was at a 1979 Cardinals-Pirates game at Pittsburgh's Three Rivers Stadium. The Stars and Stripes had been hung upside down. With the Pirates trailing, 5–0, an international distress signal was sounded. The flag was lowered and re-raised the way it should be.